Cornerstones of Freedom

The Story of
WOUNDED KNEE

By R. Conrad Stein

Illustrated by David J. Catrow III

 CHILDRENS PRESS, CHICAGO

Library of Congress Cataloging in Publication Data

Stein, R. Conrad.
  The story of Wounded Knee.

  (Cornerstones of freedom)
  Summary: Recounts events leading up to the last battle fought between white men and Indians, in which
approximately two hundred men, women, and children
of the Sioux tribe were slaughtered by the United
States cavalrymen.
  1. Wounded Knee Creek, Battle of, 1890—Juvenile
literature. [1. Wounded Knee Creek, Battle of, 1890.
2. Dakota Indians—Wars, 1890-1891.   3. Indians of
North America—Wars]   I. Catrow, David J., ill.
II. Title. III. Series.
E83.89.S74 1983   973.8'6   83-6584
ISBN 0-516-04665-9   AACR2

In 1876 the Plains Indians scored a stunning victory. A huge war party destroyed five companies of the Seventh Cavalry under the command of George Armstrong Custer. The battle took place at the Little Bighorn River. Newspaper writers later called it "Custer's Last Stand." Actually, the battle was the American Indians' last stand. Never again would the red man's power reach such heights as it did at the Little Bighorn.

After Custer's defeat, the United States Army sent powerful cavalry units into the West. Sitting Bull, one of the leaders of the Plains Indians, was forced to flee to Canada. In Idaho and Oregon, the cavalry defeated the Nez Percé tribe after a bitter winter war. At his surrender, Nez Percé Chief Joseph said, "I am tired of fighting. Our chiefs are killed. . . . The old men are dead. . . . It is cold and we have no blankets. The little children are freezing to death. Hear me, my chiefs. My heart is weak and sad. I am tired."

Chief Joseph could have been speaking for all the American tribes.

By 1880, the Indians were a beaten people. Only the Apache leader Geronimo continued to ride the warpath. He surrendered in 1886. The once feared Indian warriors were now condemned to life within the boundaries of a reservation. There they would forever taste the sting of defeat.

Throughout their history, the Indians had clung stubbornly to their religion. They believed the spirit to be more important than the body. In their time of defeat they turned more and more to their spiritual leaders. The spiritual leaders often were called medicine men. In 1889, a medicine man named Wovoka started a movement that led to tragedy on the banks of a creek called Wounded Knee.

Wovoka was a member of the Paiute tribe living in Nevada. As a medicine man, Wovoka believed he lived in two worlds. One was the everyday world where the sun rose and set and the moon crossed the skies at night. The other was the spirit world. The spirit world was difficult to reach, but it made the everyday world seem to be a shadow. In the spirit world a man acquired great knowledge, such as how to make a sick person well. And in the spirit world a man was able to look into the future.

One day in 1889, an eclipse of the sun turned a

brilliant day into sudden twilight. With the sun darkened, the medicine man Wovoka fell into a deep trance. To onlookers, he seemed near death. He burned with fever and beads of sweat rolled down his face. Suddenly he came out of the trance and said he had been lifted up to the spirit world. There he had seen a marvelous vision. The buffalo had returned to the prairies in herds that numbered in the millions. Long dead Indians had risen from their graves to ride swift ponies over the plains. And— best of all—the white man had vanished from the earth.

Wovoka had learned Christianity from the missionaries. His beliefs were a blend of Christian and Indian religions. He claimed that while he was in the spirit world he met a man very much like Christ. But this Christ figure was an Indian. The figure told Wovoka the Indians must never again wage war. Instead the red man could achieve what Wovoka saw in his vision by performing a certain dance. It was a slow, measured dance that had to be performed by entire tribes. The dance would have to last two or three days and nights. During that time, the dancers must not take food or water. If the dance were performed faithfully, the Christ figure promised, the red man would soon regain all his lost lands.

Like a prairie fire whipped by the wind, word of Wovoka's vision swept the Indian world. Whole tribes formed huge rings and performed the strange new dance. When white men asked the meaning of the dance, the Indians said it would make their dead rise from their graves. So the white men called it the "Ghost Dance."

From every corner of the West, medicine men flocked to the Paiute camp to learn the Ghost Dance. One of them was a Sioux named Kicking Bear. For hundreds of years the Sioux had been warriors and hunters. To them, staying on a reservation and trying to learn farming was agony. They thirsted to return to the hunt and to the warpath. Kicking Bear learned the Ghost Dance from the Paiutes. But the Sioux medicine man added his own interpretation to the dance. He said the dance would bring victory to the Sioux in a final, glorious war against the white man. He even said the dancers should wear special shirts with religious symbols painted on them. Kicking Bear claimed that in battle those shirts would turn to iron. No white soldier's bullet could penetrate them. Kicking Bear returned to South Dakota urging the Sioux to dance the Ghost Dance.

Leading the Sioux people was the aging chief Sitting Bull. He now lived peacefully on a reservation after a six-year exile in Canada. Sitting Bull was also a medicine man and believed in religious dances. Fourteen years earlier he had danced the exhausting Sun Dance. He had reached the spirit world. There he had beheld a remarkable vision. He had seen hundreds of white soldiers falling helplessly into the Indian camp. Just eight days later, his Indian braves had slaughtered General Custer and his men at the Little Bighorn River.

However, Sitting Bull believed that the Ghost Dance promised too much. No dance could make dead men rise from the earth. And no dance could turn cloth shirts into iron. Still, Sitting Bull allowed the Sioux people to practice the Ghost Dance. As a religious man, he felt there were many different ways to reach the spirit world.

Other Sioux chiefs also approved of the Ghost
Dance. Soon the Sioux people had come to believe
that the Ghost Dance was their own private pipeline
to God. A few Sioux men and women died after days
of constant dancing with no food or water. Others
continued dancing, believing the Ghost Dance would
work miracles.

Worried white families who lived near the Sioux reservations stayed awake late into the night. They saw Indian campfires flickering in the distance. They heard Indian whoops and hollers piercing the night silence. To them, the Ghost Dance meant the peace that had lasted more than a dozen years was about to be shattered. The settlers were terrified that harm would come to their children. Perhaps they would be forced to flee the farms they had worked so hard to build. All their ancient fears returned. They thought of Indians howling, Indians burning, and Indians killing. Once more, the specter of massacre haunted the white people of the Dakotas.

By mid-November of 1890, rumors of an Indian uprising had paralyzed the white community. Newspapers printed hair-raising stories about Indian threats to go on the warpath. So far, the Indians had done nothing more than dance. But according to the newspapers, the Sioux were pouring out of their reservations with fire in their eyes.

Finally, a young and inexperienced Indian agent sent this telegraph message from the Pine Ridge Indian Reservation to Washington:

INDIANS ARE DANCING IN THE SNOW AND ARE WILD AND CRAZY.... WE NEED PROTECTION AND WE NEED IT NOW.... THE LEADERS SHOULD BE ARRESTED AND CONFINED IN SOME MILITARY POST.

In Washington, worried generals sent the army into South Dakota. Leading the troops were units of the Seventh Cavalry, Custer's old command. It was the same regiment that had been defeated at the Little Bighorn fourteen years earlier.

Even before the army arrived, an Indian agent named James McLaughlin dreamed up a plan to break the spirit of the Ghost Dancers. Indian agents were paid by the government to help the Indians. But the Indian agency stank with corruption. Many agents stole the food and farm equipment that was supposed to go to the Indians. McLaughlin was an honest agent, but he sometimes acted like a policeman whose job was to keep the Sioux in line. His plan was simple. He wanted to arrest the Indian leaders. He hoped that would discourage the people from dancing the Ghost Dance. To begin his plan, McLaughlin ordered the arrest of the most famous of the Sioux chiefs—fifty-six-year-old Sitting Bull.

Cold moonlight glowed behind the clouds on the morning of December 15, 1890. Through the snow rode about forty horsemen. They were Sioux policemen hired by Indian agent McLaughlin. The Sioux called such Indian police "Metal Breasts" because of the badges they wore. McLaughlin hoped Indian policemen would be able to arrest Sitting Bull more easily than white policemen could.

As the Metal Breasts rode into Grand River Camp, they passed a magnificent white stallion tied up near a shed. That horse had been a gift to Sitting Bull from his friend Buffalo Bill Cody. Years earlier, Sitting Bull had been a member of Buffalo Bill's traveling Wild West show. The gift horse was trained to sit up on his hindquarters and kick his front hooves in the air whenever he heard a gunshot.

Leading the riders was a Sioux police lieutenant named Bull Head. He ordered his men to surround Sitting Bull's cabin. He then dismounted and burst through the door. He discovered Sitting Bull asleep and rolled the chief off his bed. "You are under arrest," he said. "If you fight, we will kill you."

At once, Sitting Bull realized that fighting would be useless. He told the police lieutenant he would go peacefully. He only wanted time to dress. But Bull Head and his men would not let Sitting Bull dress. Instead, they pushed the chief out of his cabin and into the snow while he was still in his underwear.

Outside, a large crowd had gathered. The people cursed at the Metal Breasts for manhandling their chief. A few of the men in the crowd carried rifles. Fearing trouble, Bull Head dragged Sitting Bull over the ground, trying to hurry him out of the village. Suddenly a shot rang out. The shot was followed by the crackling of dozens of rifles and pistols. The firing roared for five dreadful minutes. Finally, a woman screamed and pointed to the ground. Lying still, his face in the snow, was the mighty chief Sitting Bull. Also killed were eight other villagers including Sitting Bull's seventeen-year-old son, Crowfoot.

As the Metal Breasts backed out of the village, the people heard the high-pitched neighing of a stallion. Upon hearing the gunfire, the old white show horse had stood on his hindquarters and kicked his front hooves in the air. To the Sioux, this was a miracle. Their beloved chief was dead. But to honor his death, even his horse danced the Ghost Dance.

In the past, the Sioux would have gone to war over the killing of their chief. But the people were too excited about the Ghost Dance to seek revenge. To dance in peace, however, the Sioux had to be safe from the Metal Breasts and the cavalry. About one hundred of Sitting Bull's followers joined the camp of Chief Big Foot. They knew he believed in the wonders promised by the Ghost Dance. They did not know that Big Foot was one of the Indian leaders the government had ordered arrested.

When told of Sitting Bull's death, Chief Big Foot decided to join forces with a neighboring Sioux tribe. On the road to the neighboring tribe, Big Foot and his followers were spotted by a unit of the Seventh Cavalry. Big Foot was sick with pneumonia. He had been coughing up blood for two days. The chief told his group to surrender to the soldiers. The cavalry commander ordered Big Foot to set up his tepees and tents on the banks of a creek called Wounded Knee.

Wounded Knee Creek was known for two events in Sioux history. Once one of the Sioux chiefs had gashed his knee while fighting warriors of a rival Crow tribe. To escape his enemies, the chief had swum into the creek. From then on, the creek was called Wounded Knee. Also, the famous Sioux Crazy Horse was buried in a secret grave somewhere along the creek bank. Crazy Horse was one of the chiefs who had led the Sioux to victory against George Custer. Some Ghost Dancers believed that Crazy

Horse would rise from his grave and lead the Sioux to a final, glorious conquest.

At Wounded Knee camp, the soldiers counted Big Foot's people. They numbered about 120 men and 230 women and children. The first night in camp passed peacefully. The soldiers issued food to the Indians. Many of them were close to starving. A regimental doctor treated Big Foot's pneumonia. But later that night, the cavalry commander placed four Hotchkiss guns on the hills looking down on the camp. Hotchkiss guns were new, fast-firing cannons that could hurl a shell three miles. Colonel James Forsyth wanted those guns in place for tomorrow's dangerous task. Forsyth planned to take away the

Indians' weapons at dawn. He was sure the braves would not give up their arms without some kind of a struggle.

The next day an icy wind whipped out of the north and the temperature dipped below freezing. About five hundred well-armed cavalrymen completely surrounded the group of 350 Indians. The Sioux had only a few outdated rifles. Two-thirds of the Indians were women and children. No one knew that these uneven sides were about to fight the last battle in the long history of warfare between Indians and white men.

An Indian brave named Wasumaza lived to tell a writer how the day began. "The following morning

there was a bugle call. Then I saw the soldiers
mounting their horses. It was announced that all
men should come to the center for a talk.... Big
Foot was brought out of his tepee and the older men
gathered around him."

With the Indian leaders assembled, Colonel Forsyth demanded the immediate surrender of all their
weapons. The chiefs talked softly to each other.
Finally they handed over two or three broken car-
bines. Colonel Forsyth was not satisfied. He ordered
his troops to search the Indian tents, tepees, and
wagons. The soldiers barged into the shelters, tore
apart bedding, and kicked over pots and pans.
Women inside the shelters screamed. Babies cried.

During the search, a medicine man named Yellow Bird began chanting a prayer-song. He then stood and danced a few steps of the Ghost Dance.

The soldiers found no weapons inside the shelters. Colonel Forsyth became convinced the Indians were hiding their guns in their clothing. He ordered a body search of each warrior. As the soldiers moved closer, the medicine man chanted even louder. The soldiers did not understand the Sioux language. They thought he was continuing to sing his prayers. But the medicine man had changed from prayers to advice. "You have nothing to fear," he told the other warriors. "The Ghost Dance has turned your shirts into iron. No bullet can harm you."

Suddenly a brave named Black Coyote produced a rifle from under his cloak. He held it above his head and screamed at the cavalrymen. Black Coyote was deaf and had no idea what the soldiers intended to do. "If they had left him alone he was going to put his gun down," said Wasumaza. "They came on and grabbed the gun that he was going to put down. Right after they spun him around there was the report of a gun. It was quite loud."

The first shot was probably fired by a Sioux. It triggered a nightmare.

All at once, hundreds of rifles roared. "It sounded like the tearing of canvas," said one witness. Soldiers fired into the packed ranks of Indians. The Indians returned the fire with what few weapons they had. At arm's length, soldiers and Sioux hacked at each other with fists, knives, and bayonets. One of the first to die was the ailing chief Big Foot. His death spared him from seeing the horror that followed.

From on top of the hills, the four deadly Hotchkiss guns opened up on the Indian camp. Exploding shells shredded the tents and tepees. Red-hot shell splinters whistled through the air and cut down anything in their path. Women and children ran screaming out of their tepees. Shells burst in their midst. They fell, their blood reddening the snow.

The Indians tried to escape by running into the ravine that led out of camp. The soldiers followed them with rifles blazing. Then the Hotchkiss guns were pushed to a new position so they could sweep the ravine with shellfire. Later, the bodies of women and children were found more than two miles away from the campsite. They had been gunned down as if they were props used for target practice.

When the last gunshot had been fired, the soldiers

counted their losses. Twenty-nine troopers had died, and thirty-three were wounded. Since the Indians had only a few weapons, many historians have concluded that most of the soldiers were struck by their own bullets during the wild firing. No one counted the Indian dead. Later estimates put that number at about two hundred.

In the smoky camp, a Seventh Cavalry officer was heard to say, "Now we have avenged the death of Custer." It is not known whether anyone reminded the officer that Custer had died in a battle, not in a slaughter.

To add to the horror of the scene, a blizzard quickly buried the Indian bodies. A week later, a burial party found them frozen into grotesque shapes. Big Foot's body was as stiff as a statue. A local doctor named Charles Eastman arrived with the burial party. He gave this gruesome description: "A terrible and horrible sight to see. Women and children lying in groups, dead. Some of the young girls had wrapped their heads in their shawls and buried their faces in their hands. I suppose they did that so they would not see the soldiers come up to shoot them."

Immediately after the shooting, scores of Indian survivors wandered in the snow like sleepwalkers.

Most of them were women and children, and most were badly wounded. The soldiers gathered them up and put them in wagons. It was nightfall before the wagons arrived at the Pine Ridge Army Base. The army barracks were filled with soldiers, and the officers debated what to do with the Indians. Meanwhile, the survivors shivered in the open wagons. Finally, someone opened the doors of a church. The Indians crawled out of the wagons and into the church. Most of them were caked with blood. It was four days after Christmas, and a banner above the church proclaimed:

PEACE ON EARTH. GOOD WILL TO MEN.

When the news leaked out, many Americans were horrified by what had happened at Wounded Knee. General Miles, who commanded the army units in the Dakotas, was furious. He brought charges against Colonel Forsyth for allowing his men to fire on women and children. Later, the War Department dismissed the charges. Forsyth was never punished.

Why did the men of the United States Army behave so brutally at Wounded Knee? Certainly they were afraid of the Indian warriors. Memories lingered of the bloody battles fought between the Sioux and the cavalry in the past. Also, the Indians would have been wiser to surrender their arms at once while they were surrounded by such a strong force. But perhaps the attitude of the soldiers toward the Indians was an important factor at Wounded Knee. The young soldiers had grown up during the fury of Indian wars. At that time the attitude that prevailed was "The only good Indian is a dead Indian." That attitude might have led to the tragedy at the creek bank.

More than the broken bodies of Sioux people were buried at Wounded Knee. The last hope of the American Indians to recapture their old way of life died there, too. The Ghost Dance had promised a

paradise to a people living in hell. Years later, an old Sioux brave named Black Elk recalled the slaughter and said, "I did not know then how much had ended. When I look back now from this high hill of my old age, I can still see the butchered women and children lying heaped and scattered along the crooked gulch as plain as when I saw them with eyes still young. And I can see that something else died there in the bloody mud and was buried in the blizzard. A people's dream died there. It was a beautiful dream."

The "battle" also ended the long history of wars fought between the American white man and the Indian. Those wars had raged on and off almost since the two peoples had met. General Miles had eight thousand troops in the Dakotas. With this powerful army he was able to force any rampaging tribes back to their reservations. The Indians never again took to the warpath.

As the years passed, the events at Wounded Knee were remembered only by students of history. It seemed as if most Americans wanted to forget this stain on their record. Then, in 1973, a group of two hundred armed Indian militants took over the battle site and held it for two months. Two Indians died in gun battles with federal marshals. The militants claimed that they were protesting the many treaties with the Indians that the United States government had broken. Other people, including many Indian leaders, called the militants hoodlums who were trying to get their faces on television. The take-over did serve to remind Americans of a part of their history that most would rather have forgotten.

But not all Americans could forget what happened in South Dakota during the Christmas season of 1890. Some thirty years afterward, poet Stephen

Vincent Benet was living in Paris with a group of other American writers and painters. He must have been haunted by the nightmare of the massacre as he wrote a poem with these lines:

> I shall not rest quiet in Montparnasse.
> I shall not be there, I shall rise and pass.
> Bury my heart at Wounded Knee.

About the Author

R. Conrad Stein was born and grew up in Chicago. He enlisted in the Marine Corps at the age of eighteen, and served for three years. He then attended the University of Illinois, where he received a Bachelor's Degree in history. He later studied in Mexico and earned a Master of Fine Arts degree from the University of Guanajuato.

The study of history is Mr. Stein's hobby. Since he finds it to be an exciting subject, he tries to bring the excitement of history to his readers. He is the author of many other books, articles, and short stories written for young people.

Mr. Stein is married to Deborah Kent, who is also a writer of books for young readers.

About the Artist

David J. Catrow III was born in Virginia and grew up in Hudson, Ohio. He spent three years in the United States Navy as a hospital corpsman then subsequently attended Kent State University, where he majored in biology. He is a self-taught illustrator. Mr. Catrow currently lives in Hudson, Ohio with his actress wife Deborah Ann and daughter Hillary Elizabeth. The artist would like to thank Deborah for her constant support and inspiration.